soul like thunder

soul like thunder

sophia elaine hanson

CALIDA LUX
PUBLISHING

SOUL LIKE THUNDER
ISBN-13: 978-1-7321376-2-2
ISBN-10: 1-7321376-2-5
Cover Design: Docshot
Printing: Createspace
Formatting: Docshot
Illustrations: Munise Sertel (instagram.com/mns_art)
Copyright: 2018 Calida Lux Publishing

for leia

trigger warning

contents:

prelude..11

part i...15

part ii...65

part iii..127

epilogue..195

prelude:

there once was a girl with a hummingbird heart.
it beat quick and steady, rattling her ribs like a freight
train.
she was raised at the edge of the forest where the coyotes
cast their songs between the trees each night.

her father danced with her to *wonder* —
natalie merchant always sounded like home.
her mother bathed her in galaxies to remind her
to walk with her chin tipped up.

she was raised to be strong.
she was raised to be kind.
she ended up somewhere in between.

her baby teeth popped free and her legs grew long.
thunder rolled in her bones, cold as the sea and wide as
the tundra.
she opened her mouth and spit the storm at the mirror,
only to discover it was a universe in disguise.

she bunched the dark matter into ink until it was quiet.

the wolves came when she was fifteen and they kept
coming.
they came from her brain.
they came from her body.
they came from the creeping hands of a boy she had not
invited in.
they came from the boy she had planted in her belly,

who uprooted himself only to turn and call her the weed.

she was fortunate enough to be soft.
she was unfortunate enough to be soft.

she stuffed herself with brambles and ivy to shroud the
gravestone of her chest.
she tucked her head beneath the skyline and slept, too
heavy to do anything but.
she begged with a god she did not believe in not to kill
her,

but to unmake her.

there was no answer.

but the storm in disguise, the one she forced out so long
ago,
came crawling back, speaking in a language only she
could understand.

we have work to do, it says.

part i: nova

sophia elaine hanson

nova, nova
my catastrophic expansion

.

soul like thunder

you ask me
where i come
from

i tell you

i come from
everlasting arms

i come from
rocky cathedrals

i come from
the lip of the
wilderness

i come from
centuries of tundra

i come from
slow mornings

i come from
rudderless nights

i come from
waves of antiseptic

i come from
oceans of doubt

i come from
seasons of sun

— *origins*

my name was always too big for me
the third syllable was the extra space
in my winter boots to make room for
someday

two syllables and a blunt rounded end
was more manageable — my nickname
tasted like cotton candy

its mother chimed with wisdom i did
not possess

one day, i tried it on like the lab coat
my mother used to hang in the back hall
fabric bunched at my wrists and knees
but i wore it anyway

— *syllables*

my mother teaches me
not to feel shame when
my mouth goes dry at the
thought
of your hands on my waist

— *the gift*

i hope you're afraid
i hope every *me too*
is a warning shot
white hot against your
temples
i will keep you here
in limbo, knowing at
any point i could aim
and ignite

— *me too*

my first love was
ecstatic and volatile
every day i fell
so hard and fast my
skin would spider
each time he caught me
you need not catch me

— *i am already in your arms*

fingers curled around
house keys and bottles of mace
braided hair and clenched teeth
whispered warnings
against our cheeks
did you check your drink?

— *the language of women*

morning peels from the
gray like a tag from a
bodega orange

— *lower east side*

let me drag my teeth
through the smokestacks
taste the bittersweet
notes of a late spring

— *acela express*

bloom with wrath
black water lily
carry me on your breath
slip me between your tongue
and the roof of your mouth
be my roof
i'll be your floor
be my window
i'll be your door
i'll be the water
where you lie in wait
my black water lily

— *the water and the wrath*

sophia elaine hanson

someone once told me
that if you want to disappear,
all you have to do
is rent an apartment in manhattan

— *fast track to oblivion*

soul like thunder

i am not accustomed to being wanted
when my phone shivers in my back pocket
it is from shock

— *as much as elation*

there is something in
the curve of your lips,
the arch of your back,
the bend of your brow

— *that makes me think i can dance*

there is poetry
in the way you
say my name
there is verse
in the way
you hold me

— *you are better with words than you think*

the day comes
that i understand
my mother is
tragically, achingly
human

— *just like me*

my heart
has always been
winter
i sing the aria
of the high north
in plain stocky
english
then you
cracked the tundra
pulling green from
the permafrost

— *te amo / jeg elsker deg*

you

the poor little word
has been through so much

frayed and sagging
bruised and rattled
from the ones i evicted
and the ones who vacated

somehow,

you

have oiled the *y*
straightened the *o*
righted the *u*

now,

when i let the word
unfold from my tongue
all i see is

— *you*

gimme that easy sympathy
gimme the sound of your heart
the rhythm of your wounds

— *greed*

i am whole
without your hand in mine

— *i still want it there all the time*

i want your flaws
let me cradle them,
remind them they
are part of a masterpiece

— *masterpiece*

soul like thunder

you look like a prayer
that might just be answered

— *how to kneel*

we are content in the ecstatic,
fearful wilds of the unknowable
universe

— *atheists*

the weight of your lips
pressed against mine in
the blue gray blush of
dawn

the kiss of your palms
pressed against mine in
the loping stride of the
afternoon

the smell of your skin
pressed against mine in
the hungriest part of the
night

— *lips, palms, skin*

sophia elaine hanson

you never knew it, but
you cradled my mother and
fed her galaxies for breakfast
and she raised me to the moon

— *princess / general*

you say i am a real
new yorker now
mascara blacked eyes,
whiskey sharp breath,
hair mussed and matted

— *was it the dancing, or what came after*

i am a child of the in between
hung by my hair above certainty

— *between*

can we be lonely
t o g e t h e r
just you and me

— *together*

soul like thunder

hair like black tea and
eyes like hot cider, i wonder
what her mouth tastes like

— *across the platform*

girls —

cherish your edges
feed the animal in your ribs
and in the deepest part of the night
treat your soul like a robin's egg

boys —

cherish your softness
feed the animal in your ribs
and in the deepest part of the night
protect your soul like a match in the wind

and everyone in between —

cherish your beauty
feed the animal in your ribs
and in the deepest part of the night
ignite your soul like the fourth of july

— *animals, iii*

girls are necklaces tangled
at the bottom on my jewelry box
they are distance, curiosity
they are envy, desire — and i
cannot tell where one ends and the other
begins

— *girls*

i am not
    greedy
    confused
    gay
    straight
    lying
    a slut
    unfaithful
    going to let you watch

— *bisexual*

i want to go on
walkabout
in your skin
traverse
the mountain range
of your spine
swim laps
in the dark pools
of your irises

— *walkabout*

tucked into the cove
of the open mouthed
taqueria on the corner
you offer me a bite of
your meal
i bite your lip instead

— *bite*

you and i
exist in the folds of this song
anchored by the altos, swung
high by the sopranos
we tuck it into our suitcases as if
we were the ones carrying it and
not the other way around

— *honeybee*

i see you and my lungs
threaten to burst with all
the oxygen i forgot how to
breathe

— *breathless*

beneath your touch i
bloom
red and white suns
twist
into ribbons of gold
crack
with effervescent thunder
ignite
for you; all for you

— *touch*

the more i crave you
the more i fear you

— *the fear*

trømso smells like home
my senses rise up on their
tiptoes, chanting

home
home
home

can you really build a home
of ancestry and bone?

— *trømso*

you turn my face into
an abstract painting
lipstick smeared across
milky skin
charcoal thunderheads
beneath my lashes
you turn my body into
a circuit board
so turn me on

— *sex*

sophia elaine hanson

yesterday you
accidentally
called it *our* place

— *apartment*

the chain around your neck
the wink of your full moon glasses
beneath the lower east side lights
the music of that first *hello*
that loaded pause because it is
2 a.m. and we both know this
is a little wrong
is this alright
      is that okay
           how does that feel
do you want me to stay
      yes,
          yes,
              yes,
stay

   — *notes from the night we met*

people ask me about you
and i unspool a tapestry of
adjectives
funny and empathetic
kind and adventurous
enduring and selfless
because i cannot tell them
the truth

— *you are my everything*

part ii: blackhole

black hole, black hole,
claim my fraying edges

a clot of cops forms outside my bodega
on a languid sunday morning

i smile and i nod, bread and milk safe in
my canvas bag

have a nice day, ma'am
thank you

i cast my eyes to the snow — wondering
how it might have been were my skin not the same
color

— *privilege*

if he does it once,
he will do it again

— *this is your exit sign*

if she does it once,
she will do it again

— *this is your exit sign, ii*

sophia elaine hanson

what's your deepest fear

he asks me over the brim
of his tacky plastic cup
i chew my ice, swallow my truth

spiders

— men

the day comes when i am
no longer blind to the pattern

— *you are just a little much*

that night
we are drawn to the commons

silent as wraiths,

       empty as rhymes

somebody cracks a bottle
to sear away

— *election night*

i bleed out without a mark on me
you try to hold me in your palms
you might as well try to cradle the
dead sea in a teacup

— *i went too far*

he called it going dark,
when my brain flushed
everything but the shrapnel

— *going dark*

no.
no.
no.
no.
no.
no.
no.

— *i know he heard me*

disorder strikes suddenly
saunters through the door,
sits cross legged on the
kitchen table, watches me
over my cereal and toast

— *chronic*

i become

the spaces

between

its teeth,

the gaps

between

generations

— *chronic, ii*

the strings shiver before they snap; runs appear in my
skin

— *chronic, iii*

get well soon
hope you feel better
you are so brave

       i will not
       i cannot
       i am

— *i just wish i did not have to be*

almost

— *the loneliest word in the world*

sophia elaine hanson

my pain is not a gift
there is no silver lining
there is no divine plan
there is only me, my bones,
my frantic pulse

— *silver lining*

i am the hot coals
i am the edge of a kitchen knife
i am the unhallowed ground

— *unclean*

who knew emptiness could be so heavy

— *exit serotonin*

nothing is sharp and everything is heavy
i am a mile high and seven feet under the snow
i kneel in the soil and palm the earth
it smells like your skin and it feels like your sheets

— *winter and dust*

i will never forget the night
you crumbled onto my thighs
i knit my fingers in your hair
and lied

— *everything is okay*

it is drowning in a desert
it is the heaviest breath you have ever heaved
it is the moon tacked to the pale of noon
looming, unnerving, constant

— *depression*

i am rootless
a vine strung
between breathless
trees
a telephone wire
for calls to pass
between

— *rootless*

some nights, exhaustion
distracts me from sleep
it plays with me in the pale
dark, traces the curve of my
ear, drums its fingers on the
hollows of my chest, every
beat singing,
you are not enough
you are not enough
you are not enough

— *beat*

ten truths

i.   it took me two years to say the words
ii.   i was assaulted
iii.   they tasted like salt
iv.   i thought about telling her, your new girlfriend
v.   but i was afraid
vi.   six years later i still wonder if you did to her what you did to me
vii.   six years later i still wonder if it was just a little bit my fault
viii.   six years later my throat still closes when your name bubbles up on my phone
ix.   before i learned how to be a survivor i had to accept that I was a victim
x.   i had to learn how to feel anything at all

sophia elaine hanson

my body is a house
on creaking stilts, a
water spider over the
marshland
when the hurricane
season comes i'll be
driftwood again

— *unsteady*

you live in my heart

if you leave,
who will mind the
chambers

i sleep in your chest

if i leave,
who will snap your ribs
back into place

— *snap*

sophia elaine hanson

i know i am
heaving bursting crackling
with all i cannot control
i know i am
caving fraying crumbling
with all i should not know

— *stay*

i wrap solitude around my shoulders,
shut my eyes to the noise
when i am ready to shed my skin, it is too late

— *they have already moved on*

sophia elaine hanson

i think i was born lonely,
starved for platonic touch

— *starving*

you say we are out of the woods

as if i do not cross the street
to avoid packs of them

their intentions sharper than any
teeth

you say we are out of the woods

— *but all i see are trees*

i am tired of the pretty wounds i see on t.v.
coy scars, elegant illnesses, melodramatic
disasters

i swear

there is nothing holy about the war on my body

— *pretty wounds*

i cry until i make myself sick
as if i had licked salt from my fingertips
thinking it was sugar

— *12:33 a.m.*

it could have been worse
at least you weren't raped

— *after words*

but i thought
he was your boyfriend

— *after words, ii*

she broke his heart

— *after words, iii*

does that
really count

— *after words, iv*

let it go
you're over
reacting

— *after words, v*

i hope
we can

keep this
between

us

— *after words, vi*

fear burrows in my stomach
where it is warm and vulnerable
anxiety claims my chest
with plenty of bars to hang its hooks

— *claim*

on nights like this,
isolation lays out
his tools, a salesman
hawking his wares
i touch each one,
examine them in
all their glory

— *touch*

i fear the nights when
the faucet in my eyes
sputters and groans
giving way to drought

— *stifled*

sophia elaine hanson

my bones are wet dynamite
i ignite with a nudge, a kiss
of foul air

— *unstable*

you curl me under your arm
to protect me from the blast
trouble is

— *i am the bomb*

i want to hurl my rage at you
we all know my words are
ballistic
instead
i drown in quicksand of all i cannot say

— *ballistic*

am i
a devil
who wore
a disguise
so long
she forgot
her horns

— *horns*

sophia elaine hanson

but if i am
a devil
you are, too

— *horns, ii*

plastic orange
gravestones
line my vanity
here to raise my bones

— *head and heart*

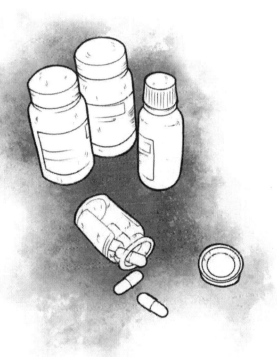

i want to flee
this fever dream
but how will i
show my face
outside these
rising borders

— *borders*

the next morning
i awoke shocked
to find the world
on fire

my friend laughed
and asked me if
i had not smelled
the smoke

— *wake up*

i dread the iridescent sting
of death and the hollow ache
of what comes after

— *dread*

sophia elaine hanson

i miss you deeper than a call can reach

— *"come home to my heart"*

(inspired by 'supercut' by lorde)

the trouble is,
we both believe
we are the one
holding us

    t o g e t h e r

— *glue*

sophia elaine hanson

i wake up in a crust
of molten rock, laid
out on white sheets

and you ask me
why i do not stand

— *bad days*

what do you become
in the eye of suffering

these hurricanes chase
each other in breathless
circles around me

i reach out

to stroke the fear from
their bowed spines but

they flinch, shiver, and
whirl away

— *the eye*

sophia elaine hanson

i would rather not be enough

— *the truth is i am too much*

the trick
is not to find someone
to sit in hell with
the trick
is to find someone
who will walk through hell
with you

— *all the way to the other side*

you stayed when
the highways of
my head crumbled
you stayed when
the bridges in my
bones buckled

— *you stayed*

sophia elaine hanson

i have endured
three endless days
packed
with insatiable seconds
hungry for my bones
the first came
when they told me
this was permanent
that in a year
i might be a girl
or i might be
a monster
the second started
in the middle of the night
when he held me down
and reminded me of
what i owed him
the third was
when you left me

— *endure*

part iii: nebula

nebula, nebula,
make me a home

i have never known peace
like your arms around me

— *11:24 p.m.*

sophia elaine hanson

sit still in your pain
let it hold you, rock you
but do not let it own you

— *still*

this is for my women with
starfall hearts and blown glass eyes

this is for my women with
broken hands and unbroken ties

this is for my women with
wild hair and ghosts in their lungs

this is for my women with
unsung mothers and wars on their tongues

this is for my women with
bruised peach skin and fear flayed nails

this is for my women with
hummingbird hearts and thighs that tell tales

of nights they found love and nights to forget
of days passed in silence, words not to regret

— *i am yours*

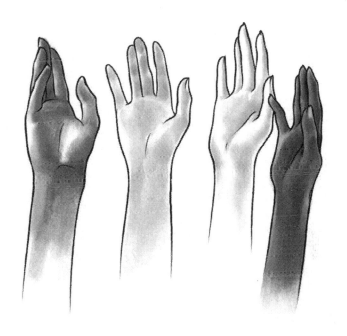

go ahead, shatter me
just mind your fingers,
my edges are not as
tender as my dear heart

— *butterfly blade*

i cannot apologize
for the words i cast
across your skin

they are the ashes of
all this world has
failed to teach me

— *unlearn*

i am not a
succubus

feeding
on the heavy
breathes of
strange men
trailing me
through the
subway

i am not an
enchantress

weaving
hexes in the
motion of my
hips beneath
my school skirt

but touch me
with your dirty
hands or your
molasses words

and i will be
your revenant

— *revenant*

i thought his touch
would never fade
now —
he is just the fog
that chases the rain

— *the fox / first love*

every day you
pull me closer,
remind me that
the threads we
have moored
at our fingers
and lips
are without end

— *mooring*

there is no grace in our afflictions.
there is only grace in the way
we lift ourselves up and walk on

— *grace*

you are so sure
that we will survive this
s e p a r a t i o n

god knows i am sure about you

but my love,
this city will be so much
hungrier
without you at my side

— *hungry*

i hope these are things
you and i laugh about
years from now

— *young and dumb*

your curls
the rose you press to my neck
the song i comb from the white noise
the scar the moon leaves on our eyelids

— *white noise*

honey could drip from the kitchen sink
and i would still say your lips were sweeter

— *ten cent kisses*

somehow,
the radiance has found its way
into every inch of your body
it bleeds through your skin
teases your curls into a halo
sugars your every word

— *radiance*

i never knew
burning pancakes with you could
smoke the past right out of me

— *smoke me out*

i will be your
ace of hearts if
you will be my
soul like thunder

— *up my sleeve*

i wish i had the words
to explain the storm
you have kicked up in
my stomach

— *speechless*

build me a fortress
of cotton and down
weave me a morning
of dew and pearls

— *make me a home*

please do not ask me to curb my love
you know i would scoop handfuls of
light from the milky way to bathe you
i can be more but darling
i will never be less

— *curb*

nobody ever tells you
love is a gamble
nobody ever tells you
love is not enough

— *the gamble*

sophia elaine hanson

you found her
someone new
pretty, a camera
around her neck
i stopped longing
for you long ago
but i have to ask

— *do you call her hummingbird, too?*

i walk tall
on the arched spine of my past

— *vertebrae*

maybe i would be lonely
tangled in the pulsing
strings of ten thousand hearts

— *vibrato*

woman is not a personality trait
i do not carry my
creativity sensitivity volatility
in the curve of my breasts or
the apex of my thighs

— *the things we carry*

sophia elaine hanson

a young god pops the fireworks
over our neighborhood
she likes the way they challenge the night,
hurl their rage at the stars

— *the fourth*

i wanted to be a dancer
to strike flint in the eyes
of a thousand watchers
to hang by my grace above
disaster

i wanted to be a dancer
and here i am; a writer

— *the dancer*

i hope you think of me
in the cold place between
day and night

not because you fill
the caverns of my chest

but because i must believe
i was more to you
than the bruises you left
on the secret parts of me

— *impressions*

your body was not woven
from the threads of frayed stars
just to be coveted
you are the god; it is the machine

— *god in the machine*

speak easy

pick your skeletons apart,
lay the pieces before me

i cannot rearrange them
i cannot give them skin

but i can listen
to how they came apart

how you
how i
can put them back together

— *speak easy*

we are both
fatally,
devastatingly
human

— *fatal*

some mornings
i wake up with a barbed wire tongue
and there you are with your fawn soft
skin
and there you are with your peach blossom
eyes

— *barbed wire*

some mornings
you wake up with broken bottle teeth
and there i am with my petal soft
hands
and there i am with my velveteen
eyes

— *glass*

pain is rarely temporary
and always reactionary
it lingers like a bad cough
shivers at the slightest touch
light it up and you will sear
away your skin
treat it like a child and it will
find a soft corner to sleep

— *handle with care*

sophia elaine hanson

we strip your apartment
you bandage the wounds
in the white bricks
i scrape the days from the tub

your bedroom breathes in
the last gasps of summer
and i tell you your next
place will be our place

— *our place*

when hate becomes the norm
love itself becomes resistance

— *resist*

can we be brave
t o g e t h e r
just you and me

— *together, ii*

tell me where it hurts
i will kiss it with my words
show me where you bleed
i will stitch it with my veins

— *bandaid*

ground me, my love
who wants to be a bird
in a sky so cold

anchor me, my love
who wants to be a ship
in a sea so mad

— *the bird and the sea*

does smoke feel fear
when it unfurls from the
loving embrace of a
cigarette

— *the last time i left his house*

visit your demons
in the marshy lowlands
buried deep within your
stomach

— *but do not live there*

sophia elaine hanson

this beast
it steals from you, too
and calls it generosity

and oh, is it generous

you are dripping with
privilege, robed in power

and my god, how i want
to break your brutal crowns

but i see the taking, too

i see the taking in the boys
choking on poetry, strangled
by their own softness

i see the taking in the boys
clinging to their lovers in
the secrecy of their bedrooms

i see the taking in the boys
leashed by ignorance, cowering
at the headstone of tradition

— *feminism is for all of us*

boys can be abused
boys can be assaulted

— *there is no 'too'*

i can shoulder the weight of
any injustice pressed onto me
but if they touch *you*

        god help them

— *better start praying*

i carry in me the seed of grit
careful, push me to the dirt and
i will bloom with wrath

— *grit*

my thumb hovers over your name.

not 'baby.' not 'love.' no more pet names. just your name. the one that was once holy to me.

what is there to say

when you nearly burned? when your mattress — the one that sags in the middle — is dust?

i wonder if i would have felt you wink out of existence.

it is selfish, really. i know you are glazed with shock. i know you are taking care of

yourself
your family
your girl

but i need to be sure that before
one of us is in the ground, before
history has steeped us in apathy,

you know i forgive you
and i wish you all the peace

that has blossomed in me.

— *your house burned*

love and evolution
howl through the
halls of our history
i run with them
i crawl through them
i bow to them and
god,
how i howl for them

— *"endless forms most beautiful and wonderful"*

(inspired by 'on the origin of species' by charles darwin)

selflessness,
is stroking a shivering heart
while your own cries like a
wounded animal

— *wounded*

why do you write
for fear of silence
why do you write
for fear of noise

— *deafening*

why do we talk about love and life
is if they were separate entities

— *symbiotic*

i see you in the small
moments not meant for
my tired eyes

she touches his knee
i cradle your ghost

he takes his hand
i lace my fingers

she kisses her forehead
i sing your absence to sleep

— *distance*

sophia elaine hanson

your windowsill
on the cusp of a
new york summer
legs over the edge
of this four story
walkup
the heat presses
down
from above and
up
from below
look, lover
somebody has
cracked
the hydrant
come on,
lover, the city
has rolled into
one last crescendo
just for you

— *your last week in the city*

you and me
we are the fog horn
across the sound
we are the thyme
rolled between fingertips
we are the thick stillness
before a thunderstorm

— *soul like thunder*

whoever said love was a dance
must have been punch drunk on
their own ego

love is a glass shattering on rewind
a million little pieces tugged into a
tight embrace

— *we break, we heal*

sophia elaine hanson

that softness you try to bury
crown yourself with it and
lift your quivering chin

— *velveteen*

your voice wraps around me
three blocks from my place
and i am already home

— *home*

i know you would
pluck at your heartstrings just
to play me a sweet melody

i know you would
patch the holes in the night sky just
to help me sleep

now,

let me pull you from the deep

— *stitches*

the best loves are the messiest
i am learning this the hard way
i am
teaching myself how to shrink and bloom,
to hoard my words and spill them on the
kitchen floor,
all to the rhythm of your irregular pulse
you watch me blunder, you see my fall
please,
grant me your hand, remember you too
have skinned your knees at my feet

— *messy*

the future
expands before us
frail as a baby bird
vast as the noble sky
unknowable
as your heart or mine

— *take my hand*

epilogue:

i wrote the majority of these poems in the midst of the exquisite, flawed, electric relationship i laid before you. not long after the final stanza fell into place, that relationship ended.

a part of me wanted to scrap this entire collection.

another part of me wanted to alter it, to add another section filled with agony and guilt and fear and betrayal.

in the end, i chose to leave it as is.

it is a time capsule. a monument to one of the most important relationships i have ever had. not my first love, but my deepest.

if there is one thing i have learned in my measly twenty-one years it is that love does not begin and end with a single person. you cannot hunt it down. but it will come to you. not the same love. it will touch and taste and smell foreign until it is familiar and then all at once — it is home.

i will have that again. so will you.

acknowledgements:

to my mom and dad — thank you so much for everything you have done to support me. from my career to my health to my heartbreak. i love how close we are, and i never want that to change.

to my fellow poets — amanda lovelace, cyrus parker, morgan nikola-wren, gretchen gomez, anne chivon, cheyenne raine, and so many more. i am so lucky to have you in my life. you are all so talented, and i am just glad to be around catching some of the light coming off you. and yes, that was a *treasure planet* reference.

to my friends and loved ones — allie wolters, sarah maggard, maya, rich, and tracey lippard, mackenzie shrieve, alana cohen, cass moskowitz, beverly tan, dani hristev, annmarie morrison, jeff wu, kosyo lafchis, zoe lewis, jennifer wilson, and so many more. please know that your love and support mean the world to me. i carry you all in my heart.

to my family — words cannot express how much i love and treasure every single one of you.

to my readers — i cannot even begin to thank you for everything you have done for me. every picture, every piece of fanart, every comment, every letter makes me glow. thank you all so much.

and last, to my soul like thunder — it was real for me. it was messy and it was good and it was bad and it was wonderful. i would not take back a second of it. thank you for loving me. i will move on. you will move on. but you will always be my soul like thunder.

all the moon and all the stars,

sophia

about the author:

sophia is the author of the #1 bestselling *vinyl trilogy* as well as *soul like thunder* and *hummingbird*, two books of poetry. she loves star wars and hates cantaloupe. she currently resides in new york city where she attends her dream school, nyu.

reviews are so important to indie authors. if you enjoyed this book, please consider leaving a brief review on amazon.

Made in the USA
Columbia, SC
06 May 2018